tredition®

From Vegetable Plot To Plate

A simple practical guide to the mechanics of allotment gardening using seasonal vegetables to create rustic tasty vegetable recipes

By Debbie Hiley

© 2019   Debbie Hiley

Cover, Illustrations: Debbie Hiley

Publisher: tredition

ISBN
Paperback   ISBN   978-3-7497-7407-4
Hardcover   ISBN   978-3-7497-7408-1
eBook   ISBN   978-3-7497-7409-8

From Vegetable Plot To Plate

A simple practical guide to the mechanics of allotment gardening using seasonal vegetables to create rustic tasty vegetable recipes

By Debbie Hiley

Contents

Introduction

My interest and enthusiasm in gardening and cooking have spanned over many years, by writing this book I am combining these two interests. Growing allotment plot vegetables through the seasons accompanied by some of my favourite seasonal vegetable recipes.

Having been a vegetarian for thirty years and most recently a pescatarian I have always preferred the wonderful taste of home-grown vegetables as the taste is second to none, wonderful flavours on a plate. The finished product may not be the most attractive looking vegetable that you have ever seen but I assure you it makes up for this in taste alone. Growing good food for me was the main purpose of having an allotment plot.

I am now retired from my career as a paediatric nurse which spanned over thirty-six years. Although I do feel that this has provided me with a good foundation as it contributed somewhat to me being able to attend my allotment plot by providing me with the available time in between shifts and nurturing the patience required which has enabled me to be able to commit to and attend to it.

Having an allotment plot is a great hobby which is also very relaxing, creative, rewarding and at the same time challenging. Never the less it is always a joy to tend to, nurture and enjoy the rewards of your personal efforts. There is a great sense of community. You can join in with social banter with other allotment holders or alternatively you may prefer solitary time to yourself, it can be as interactive as you want it to be. Not only is there the added bonus of fresh air and exercise, but there is also an overall sense of wellbeing, so it is great for holding the mind body and soul together. With the ultimate goal of having the achievement and fulfilment of growing and harvesting your own delicious tasting vegetables.

In the present climate where land is being acquired for building developments, plot holders have had to take a political stand to prevent their land from being used in this way. In the village that I reside in, we needed to take this very approach, as the threat of building a small development on some of the allotments was proposed. I am happy to report that we were successful in preventing this proposition from happening. Community spirit prevailed in the end, and it was a positive outcome for the allotment holders.

More recently in 2018, the future of our allotments have been protected by the introduction of a key strategy for services and facilities in villages, with the implementation of a village plan. The idea being, that any future proposed developments for a village, should take into consideration the local village plan and remain within its framework. These plans will become part of the strategic development plan produced by district councils and, therefore, will carry weight in the determination of planning applications.

Allotments are an environmental asset, firstly creating a green space for numerous wildlife species and secondly providing a sense of community and well being for the plot holders themselves.

Over the last fifteen years I have tended my allotment plot with a fair amount of success and also with some failures along the way. It can be a ride of highs and lows. On balance a great learning curve. I will share my experience and tips for growing vegetables, which stems from trial and error and shared tips from other passionate allotment plot holders. My main aim of this book is to provide a practical guide to creating and enjoying your own plot.

Getting Started

Finding an allotment

Getting started and finding an allotment plot mainly depends on where you live in relation to it. To make it achievable you need to be reasonably close to it so that you are not travelling too far. A good starting point is to check with your local authority, the parish or borough as most allotments are council owned. Some may be privately owned by churches or local organisations and businesses. It is always a good idea to talk to one of the existing tenants on the allotment plots that you are considering to rent. The annual rent can vary according to the plot area, site, facilities, and ownership.

The best time to take on an allotment plot is the beginning or end of the year. This then allows you the time to prepare the ground in readiness for the allotment calendar year and maintains your enthusiasm and interest to continue. Once you have decided that you would like to have a go you do need to act as soon as possible as most local authorities have a waiting list for allotment plots. It is dependent on how high the demand is as to whether you will be able to take on a plot right away.

The best advice that I can give to anyone wishing to take on a plot is to share a plot when getting started. Check the tenant agreement as some authorities do not allow for sub-letting of a plot. If sharing, this allows you to get a taste for the planning and work involved on a smaller scale. After tending a shared plot, you can then decide whether this is the right size for you, it is dependant and to suit your own personal needs.

If you are given the opportunity to share an existing allotment holders plot as I was, I do think that this is by far one of the best situations to find yourself in, so that you find out what it is all about. This is how I started off initially, my lovely allotment neighbour Den allowed me to work an area of his allotment. After a couple of years I was still serious enough to continue and needed more room to grow and so took on a full allotment when it became available. This gave me a taste for what was involved and conveniently, advice was always to hand. This opportunity also gave me a taster for what I was letting myself in for. So what are you waiting for, take the plunge, jump in and give it a go.

Factors to consider

There are many factors to consider when contemplating the idea of having an allotment, I must admit I was wearing my rose tinted glasses before I acquired my very overgrown plot. The time and effort we put in at the beginning was backbreaking, but well worth the physical effort when you get to taste the end result on your plate.

These considerations are better broken down into two main groups, both personal factors and plot factors.

Personal – time, commitment, motivation, physical capability and cost.

Plot – Location, cost, site position, size of plot, type of soil, and tenant agreement.

Personal

Time - It is possible to attend a plot with a minimum of a weekly visit. Although you will have to attend more often when regular watering and harvesting is needed.

Commitment - Regular care is needed to keep on top of routine tasks, you decide how much, little or how often you do them.

Motivation – What are your aims and what do you want to achieve, and be aware of your strengths and limitations.

Physical capability – Basic physical capability is an advantage as Some of the ground work can be strenuous.

Cost – The overall cost depends on how you want to approach the plot and what funds you have available. If you already have tools the expense is reduced.

Plot

Location – The location of the plot is important, a short travelling distance and close proximity to home is helpful and more achievable.

Cost – Plot prices do vary dependant on your location and facilities available to you.

Site position – It is always advisable to check out the plot position in relation to its access points, water source, and availability of light and shade.

Size of plot – Size matters, the size is dependant on what you feel you are capable of managing. Sharing a plot initially is always a good idea.

Type of soil – Determining what type of soil you have either heavy or light, allows you to work with and improve the condition of. This will assist in growing the type of vegetables you want to grow productively.

Tenant agreement – The tenant agreement outlines your responsibilities and duties to maintain the plot in good cultivation in respect to adjoining neighbours.

Planning the Plot

Devise a plan

Start by devising a plan of your allotment plot. On your first visit to the allotment make a rough sketch plan of the layout with the position of all the important features like paths or sheds. Look at the plot and consider the layout in relation to any sloping or shady areas as this will affect what you will be able to grow in these areas. Then when you get home you can draw up the plan and mark out and allocate the beds or patches for the vegetable groups that you want to grow.

Boundaries and paths

Boundaries and paths are important as they mark out the shape of the plot and provide a means to be able to access it. A previous tenant may have already put paths in place, if this is the case, all you need to do is make sure that these work for your plan. If paths are not in place you will need to think about your access points to make them the most practical solution.

The most common material used is grass, but you may find gravel or bark a more practical solution and this also lends itself to less maintenance. There may only be one or two existing paths dividing your plot from the one next door. These paths are probably shared and will need negotiation with your neighbour to make any changes to improve or change materials for them. Paths between beds can be narrow and difficult to access.

The path between my neighbouring allotment plot was uneven and narrow so after discussion with my neighbour we removed it to allow for maximum growing space. Paths within the plot are usually your responsibility, the upkeep of the main access beds to the allotment plots usually being the responsibility of the local authority or owner.

Make sure that you are familiar with the boundaries of your plot. Hedges surrounding your allotment plot are usually your responsibility to maintain within your plot, while the outside is usually maintained by the local authority or owner. These responsibilities should be outlined in your tenant agreement.

Layout and Facilities

Consider the layout and decide whether you want raised beds or alternatively flat beds divided into patches. The advantage of having a raised bed system means that you do not have to bend too much, so less physical exertion is involved. The disadvantage is that the available growing space is reduced and the added cost involved using materials unless you use donated materials that you can recycle. Using donated materials is what an allotment is all about, reducing cost and giving some unwanted item a new lease of life, often providing a quirky one- off feature for your plot.

Think about facilities that you may want to include now or for the future such as a seating area, a shed or tool storage container, cold frame or greenhouse. Check with the tenant agreement for your local authority which will outline bye-laws for keeping livestock such as bees and chickens.

Crop Rotation

This plan then lends itself to formulating the template for your ongoing crop rotation for the next three years to complete the crop rotation cycle, ensuring that the same vegetable is not grown in the same place in successive years. Most common crop rotation groups are roots, brassicas and legumes.
Providing you have space, another bed can be added for other crops that you wish to grow. Rotation helps to avoid problems with pests and diseases by interrupting their life cycle and prevents depletion of soil nutrients. A good tip is to write on your plan the date when you have sown a crop so that you are aware of when germination should take place, this then allows you time to re-sow if you were unsuccessful the first time.

YEAR 1

LEGUMES

Peas - Broad Beans - French -

Runner Beans

BRASSICAS

Cauliflower - Broccoli - Cabbage -

Kale - Sprouts

ROOTS

Carrots - Beetroot - Parsnip -

Swedes - Potatoes

Traditionally crop rotation is divided into three main plant groups, Roots, Legumes and brassicas.

Other crops can be fitted in between, or you can create another bed. Potatoes and onions, also squashes and courgettes, work well in seperate beds.

Rotation of plant groups avoids the build up of pests and diseases and achieves a balance of nutrients in the soil that meets the different needs of each group.

The idea being that the crops rotate until they return to the first bed in the plan.

YEAR 2

BRASSICAS Cauliflower - Broccoli - Cabbage - Kale - Sprouts	

ROOTS Carrots - Beetroot - Parsnip - Swedes - Potatoes	

LEGUMES Peas - Broad Beans - French - Runner Beans	

YEAR 3

ROOTS

Carrots - Beetroot - Parsnip -

Swedes - Potatoes

LEGUMES

Peas - Broad Beans - French -

Runner Beans

BRASSICAS

Cauliflower - Broccoli - Cabbage -

Kale - Sprouts

Preparation of your plot

Once you have your plan you can then concentrate on preparing your plot. The amount of work involved depends entirely on what state the plot was in when you inherited it.

My plot was very overgrown when I took it on. Undeterred, enthusiastic and maybe a little naive we decided to knock the plot into shape. This plot was not for the faint hearted a hard-core approach was definitely needed. It was so overgrown we hired a flame thrower to burn all the brambles and weeds off to ground level and then luckily our neighbour who was a farmer, ploughed the entire area which was a great head start for us. The smell of burning could be detected two miles outside the village boundary! Having this help to get started with was a real bonus, and if you find that you are in a similar position, ask for assistance. With the goodwill of a neighbour, they are often only too happy to help out. Remnant weeds were then removed and horse manure dug in to the plot. Due to the ground being left unattended for a number of years we took advice from our allotment neighbours and grew mainly potatoes in it the first year to assist in conditioning the soil.

Digging or rotavating the plot in winter is an excellent time to plan and prepare the plot prior to sowing or planting out vegetables in spring. This together with winter frosts enables the soil to break down and become more manageable. This is also a good time to dig in manure or well- rotted compost and feed the soil to get ahead in preparation for the next years growing season.

Rotavating is quick and efficient but does have the disadvantage of cutting through weeds with long roots and multiplying them, so try and remove these beforehand. Digging is more time consuming but gives an overall better finish and texture to the soil.

Digging with a spade to a spade depth and leaving the turned over soil on top to break down, does give a finer finish and provides a better overall soil condition. This will provide the perfect medium for sowing seeds directly into in spring. The benefits of digging over the plot will become apparent over time as the soil texture improves.

When carrying out this groundwork a good tip is to allocate a two hour time slot with rests in between to reduce the strain on your back, and most importantly to make time for that all important cup of tea or a chat with a neighbour.

Improving and feeding the soil will have long term benefits whether you choose the organic or inorganic route. The soil will retain nutrients and your plants will be able to resist pests and diseases more readily.

Deciding on the way that you are going to approach and manage your allotment is entirely an individual process and the choice is yours, between using an organic system or using inorganic fertilizers. In time results will dictate which method feels right for managing your own allotment.

Tools and equipment

Tools and equipment do need to be easily accessible and stored securely. There are many secure containers, sheds, or outbuildings that can be obtained second hand or in a sale or auction for a reasonable price. A good source can be your local tip, but be prepared as you will need to be able to take it away yourself.

To begin with you will need a good set of garden tools, a spade, fork, rake, hoe, secateurs, trowel, garden trug and a watering can. A dibber is useful and a mattock especially if you have clay soil.

I made good use of an old fork handle by making a dibber from it, and kept the handle long to minimise the amount of time I was bending when using it. A line marker for marking out lines to grow your veg in rows, can easily be made from a couple of sturdy pieces of wood and securing your string to these. Buying cheap tools is a false economy as they will not last the test of time and probably not perform well. A rotavator is useful if you have a large allotment plot to prepare, but this is not essential.

If you decide to have a cold frame, but again this is not essential, this can be made easily from old wooden window frames for minimum effort and cost. As time passes you will have a better idea of what you want to achieve and what you need and require to achieve this.

Sowing seeds

Now after all the ground work and preparation here comes the exciting bit, sowing your seeds. It is always good to compare with other allotment holders to find out what vegetables are the most successful for the type of soil and climate conditions that you have. The plot is available for growing almost anything you choose.

Follow the instructions on the seed packet. According to what you want to grow, bear it in mind to have vegetables in succession, so that you do  not have a glut all at once. Plan vegetables so that you are harvesting at different times. At first you will be tempted to sow all the seeds in the first season, try and hold back if you can and save some for the following year, this prevents you having a glut and saves on the pennies too.

Seeds germinate better when they are sown into a fine tilled soil. Bear this in mind and when you look at your plan you can factor this in when preparing the ground in winter and prepare beds specifically for sowing seed into. If the weather is too cold or wet sow seeds into seed trays or plugs to get a head start and then you can plant out when it is warmer.

Watering

Watering seeds and plants is essential for their survival and growth. It is an advantage but not essential to have a water source close by. If you find that you are some distance away from the available water source, you

can always place a water butt on or near to your plot to ease the process of watering your plants.

Water butts can be purchased, alternatively you can pick a container up for free if you are resourceful enough. Look around, its amazing what people will throw away, which you can then find a use for and upcycle. If you decide to do this it is always a good idea to cover the water butt with a lid. Firstly to protect wild-life and secondly to prevent

debris and leaves from falling in, so helping to keep the water clean. If you choose to use a water butt on your allotment, a good tip is to give it a spring clean before filling it up and starting to use it.

A large container can double up to provide a useful water butt, but you will need to check the size though as it needs to be big enough to accommodate your watering can, thus allowing you to access the water easily to be able to water your plot with little effort. Having a good capacity watering can with a rose on it that provides a good shower is beneficial for watering seedlings and plants. During hot spells watering can become a full-time job and you need to be prepared for this. Check with your tenant agreement as some local authorities may not allow hose pipes to be used during hot spells.

Weeding and maintenance of the plot

Although weeding overall is not very exciting as it is quite a boring task, it is an essential task to carry out and maintain your plot. Together with maintenance of boundary hedges and plot paths which also falls into this category. In carrying out these tasks you are maintaining your tenant agreement in keeping the plot in a state of good cultivation in respect to adjoining neighbours.

Vegetables are quickly ruined if in direct competition from weeds. Weeds can quickly take hold as vegetables are grown in widely spaced rows. Most weeds are easily removed with a hoe, using regular short intervals to keep weeds at bay usually works best.

Supplementary feeding your vegetables is often worthwhile, organic or inorganic fertilisers are available, the choice is yours.

On my allotment, I am not too concerned with its appearance, a little rough around the edges suits the overall feel that I am trying to achieve. When it is fully up and running though, I am very proud of how it looks and it feels very relaxing when I am attending to it or just sitting enjoying the view with a well- earned cup of tea. I can not stress enough the need to take time out to chat, relax, take a back break, or just admire your efforts. Whatever the need, enjoy!

Compost

Compost is the wonderful end product that is created from the breakdown of material that we provide from household and garden waste. This is a very important part of recycling because it not only provides food for our plants but it saves on money, time and energy too. The best thing about having an allotment is that you will have plentyful material to add to your compost heap.

Composting is a very straightforward process, though to speed things up a little a good tip is to cut your waste into small pieces, this is key to creating compost more quickly. Eventually the materials will decompose and turn into compost under its own steam.

You will find that your garden waste will make up the bulk of the compost heap. Grass cuttings, leaves, hedge trimmings, old and dead plants, prunings, old compost, paper, vegetable peelings and tea bags, are the main ingredients of my compost bin. I avoid adding other food waste to the heap, as this can attract vermin. Your garden waste will take about three months to fully decompose. The top section of the heap will take the longest to decompose as this is the coldest section. After three months you will be ready to remove two thirds of the heap that has turned into compost. The top section can then be placed at the bottom of a new heap to start all over again.

Compost bays are easy to construct and make it easy for the transfer of garden waste from a wheel barrow to the heap. Wooden pallets are widely available secondhand and make excellent materials for compost bays by joining the pallets at ninety degree angles. You can decide how big you want your heap to be according to the space you have to site it. Alternatively various compost bins are available to buy.

Growing Spring Vegetables

Spring Vegetable Recipes

Salad Leaves and Lettuce

There is nothing better than fresh salad leaves or crisp lettuce to add texture, colour and flavour to your salad. Salad leaves are especially valuable as a cut and come again crop.

Sowing

Choose a sunny or semi-shaded spot on your plot. Salad leaf and lettuce seeds can be sown directly into the ground from March until August.

Rake the soil to a fine tilth then mark out where your seed drill is to go with a taut garden line. Using the edge of your hoe, make a drill to the depth of 1cm (1/2in) deep then sow the seeds thinly along this with a row spacing of 30cm (12in) apart. Now you can cover the drill with soil and level off with the back of your rake, pressing down lightly. Now you are ready to water the salad leaves or lettuce seeds that you have set and finish off by marking their position at the end of your row. I find old canes useful for this purpose. This serves two purposes, firstly it helps you to remember where you have sown your seeds and secondly it helps to accommodate planting of other seeds and crops into your plan. You may need to protect from slugs.

A good tip for a regular supply is to sow short rows of seeds every few weeks.

Growing

It is always important to keep Lettuces moist, water well and this will prevent them bolting. You may need to protect from slugs. When the first leaves appear, if growing in rows you can start to thin out the seedlings to 30cm (12in) apart, if growing in modules one seedling per module.

Harvesting

Pick salad leaves regularly when big enough, to prevent bolting and cut lettuces with a knife below the lowest set of leaves once big enough.

Salad (Spring) Onions

Spring onions, whether you choose either the white or red variety, are equally delicious. All varieties can be left in the ground for a longer period of time and they will develop into a small maincrop onion. A versatile vegetable as a basic ingredient for most dishes.

Sowing

Choose a sunny position, spring onion seeds can be planted straight into the ground from March to July, sow in succession.

Rake the soil to a fine tilth and mark out your line where your seed drill is to go with a taut garden line. Using the edge of your hoe, make a drill to a depth of 1cm (1/2in) deep, leaving a 10cm (4in) space between rows, now sow the seeds thinly along the drill. Now you can cover the drill with soil and level off using the back of your rake, pressing down lightly.

Now you are ready to water the spring onion seeds that you have set and then finish off by marking the line with a marker at the end of the row you have set. If sowing in succession you can sow a quarter or half a row at a time, a good tip is to mark the end of this line so that you know where to begin sowing from next time.

Growing

Once germination has taken place and the seedlings are large enough, thin out lightly to allow room for the bulbs to grow. Spring onions only need watering if the weather is dry, they may also need the occasional feed. Also make sure that they are kept weed free to reduce direct competition.

Harvesting

Once the bulbs are fully developed, they will start to push themselves out of the ground, outer leaves may yellow slightly, they are ready to harvest.

Radishes

Radishes are one of the fastest crops to grow from seed, they can germinate as quick as a month if the conditions are right. They come in a range of root shapes and sizes, round, oblong, short or long. Varieties of colours are available from white, pink, red to bi-coloured.

Sowing

Choose a sunny or semi-shade position. Radishes can be sown from March to August.

Rake the soil into a fine tilth and mark out your line where your seed drill is to go with a taut garden line. Using the back of your hoe make a drill 1cm (1/2in) deep, water the drill before sowing, this will help keep the soil moist which is what radishes tend to prefer. Sow seeds thinly along the drill, the large seed size assists this and reduces the need to thin out later. A good tip is to sew radishes in succession , about every three weeks, as they grow so quickly. Water well in and mark your row with a marker.

Growing

Radishes prefer moist soil, if they dry out, they become hollow or woody and can develop splits on the outer skin, for this reason you will have more success with them if you grow them from spring / early summer. For sewing in succession, sow every three weeks. You may need to protect from slugs.

Harvesting

Radishes are ready when they push themselves out of the ground slightly, you will see when the roots are large enough. Pick them regularly when they are young and succulent, this helps to prevent bolting.

Asparagus

Asparagus is a perennial vegetable that develops into a decorative fern, it will be one of the most interesting and attractive vegetables on your plot.

Sowing

Choose a sunny, well drained site, with shelter from strong winds. Planting 1-2yr old crowns is beneficial as raising them from seed is time consuming. Ideally prepare the bed in autumn before planting in spring. Dig a trench 30cm (12in) wide by 20cm (8in) deep, work compost and equal parts of sharp sand and grit into the base of the trench. Then use the excavated soil to create a mounded ridge down the length of the trench. After the crowns have been soaked in water place them on top with the roots spread out, leave 40cm (16in) between each plant and row, lightly cover over the crowns with soil. Water well and mulch well with compost.

Growing

During the growing season keep the asparagus bed well watered, feed in spring with a general purpose fertiliser and keep the bed weed free. A good tip is to protect the growing ferns with a cane and string support system around the bed when the ferns have formed for the first 2-3 years.

The first spears will appear 3-4 weeks after planting, it is important that these are not cut, but allowed to develop into ferns throughout the summer. These can then be cut back just above ground level in autumn when they have started to die back. Before the new spears appear in subsequent years , make a ridge of soil over each row and apply general purpose fertiliser. Avoid picking the spears in the second year too, as the plant should be left to develop a robust crown before you begin cutting the spears in the third year, but well worth waiting for.

Harvesting

Harvest when the spear is 15-20cm (6-8in) long by cutting with a knife just below the surface.

Herbs

Herbs are so decorative and versatile and a main staple for cooking in my kitchen. They add a wonderful flavour during cooking and add a different dimension to a dish when added fresh. You will be rewarded by a fabulous fragrance and a feel good factor as their aroma is released when picking them.

Sowing

There are numerous ways in which you can grow herbs. In pots, hanging baskets, containers, window boxes, or a dedicated herb patch.
Sow in spring, using a greenhouse or windowsill, sprinkling the seed thinly on the surface of the compost in a tray or pot, water well, keep moist but not too wet and label.

Growing

When the seedlings start to grow and are big enough to pot on, transfer them singly, to a small pot and grow them on until they are ready to plant out. Harden the seedlings off for a week by simply putting outside in a sunny, sheltered spot during the day and bring them in overnight. Then transfer them to their final growing position in a container or in the ground. Check the growing instructions on the seed packet and group herbs together that prefer similar conditions.

Transplant into a well drained, sunny site, adding equal amounts of compost and grit will help with the soil structure and assist with drainage as most herbs do not like to sit in wet soil. For those herbs that prefer a rich soil, prepare an area seperately, individual containers or a seperate section of a herb patch work well for this. A supply near to your kitchen will ensure fresh picked herbs are always to hand.

Harvesting

A good tip is to pick herbs regularly as this ensures that you have the luxury of a constant supply to add to your cooking and also stops the plant from producing flowers and going to seed.

Salad leaves with Blue Cheese, Celery, Apple, Sultanas and Walnuts

Serves 4

Large handful of assorted Salad leaves, washed and air dried
200g Blue cheese, crumbled
4 Sticks of celery, chopped
2 Large handfuls of walnut halves
4 Pink lady apples
Sqeeze of lemon juice
Large handful of sultanas
Dressing - 4 tablespoons Balsamic vinegar, 1 tablespoon olive oil

Wash the salad leaves and leave to air dry.
Peel, core and thinly slice the apples and mix with a squeeze of lemon juice.
Arrange the salad leaves on a plate and sprinkle the walnuts, celery, sultanas, apples and blue cheese over the top.
Add the dressing ingredients to a jam jar and shake to mix up, drizzle this over the top when you are ready to serve.

Try this accompanied with chunky coleslaw

Spring onion, and Potato Rosti

Serves 2

6 Spring onions, chopped finely, reserve some for garnishing
3 medium potatoes, skins on and quartered
2 Tablespoons Rapeseed oil
Sea salt and ground black pepper
1 Clove of garlic, peeled and crushed finely
Handful of flat leaf parsley, coursley chopped to garnish
Flaky sea salt to garnish

Part cook the potatoes in a pan of salted water for 6 minutes and drain.
When the potatoes are cool, peel them and grate them coursley.
In a bowl mix together the spring onions, potatoes, garlic and salt and pepper.
Reheat the oil in the pan until it is hot.
Add a large spoonful of the mixture at a time, flatten them down lightly and do not move them in the pan for about 5 minutes. Add no more than 3 at a time to ensure there is room for them to cook properly.
Cook until the edges are crispy and brown, then turn over with a fish slice and cook on the other side for about 5 minutes.
Drain on kitchen paper.
Garnish with the parsley, flaky sea salt and a few rings of spring onion and serve.

Try this on its own with a pickle or accompanied with a poached egg and sauted mushrooms

Raddish, Red Onion, Tomato and Avocado Salad

Serves 4

18 Medium sized raddishes
A small red onion
15 Cherry tomatoes
1 Avocado
Juice of a lime
¼ Teaspoon salt
Flat leaf parsley to garnish

Wash, dry and finely chop the raddishes and place them in a bowl.
Finely chop the tomatoes and onion and add them to the raddishes and combine together.
Peel and chop the avocado into small chunks and add to the other ingredients.
Squeeze the lime juice over the ingredients, and combine together.
Chill for 20 minutes and just before serving add the salt.
Garnish with fresh flat leaf parsley.

Try this accompanied with a wedge of lime to squeeze on top and toasted pitta bread

Asparagus, Courgette and Pea Rissotto

Serves 4

200g Rissotto rice
2 Cloves of garlic, peeled and finely chopped
100mls Dry white wine
50g Butter
75g Parmesan cheese
Sea salt and ground black pepper
450g Asparagus chopped, 2 courgettes sliced, 300g peas
3 Shallots, ½ head celery, finely chopped
1 Tablespoon Olive oil
1 Litre hot water and a vegetable stock cube
Chopped flat leaf parsley

Mix the Hot water with the stock cube in a jug.
Heat the olive oil in a pan, add the shallot, celery and a pinch of salt and sweat the vegetables for 3 minutes.
Add the garlic, after a minute add the rice, stir continuously for 2 minutes, until the rice is translucent.
Add the wine and once it has cooked in to the rice add the first ladle of stock and salt and pepper and reduce the heat to a slow simmer.
Add the chopped asparagus, courgette and peas.
Keep adding ladelfuls of stock, stir once and then allow each ladelful to be absorbed before adding the next.
Check that the rice is cooked, check seasoning, remove from the heat and add the butter and parmesan, garnish with parsley.

Try this accompanied with a wedge of lemon to sqeeze on top and crusty bread

Herb Roasted Mediteranean Vegetables

Serves 4

6 Peppers, assorted colours
3 Courgettes
2 Aubergines
3 Red onions
20 Cherry tomatoes
4 Tablespoons Olive oil
Handful of basil, rosemary, thyme and parsley
Sea salt and ground black pepper

Preheat the oven to 200 C/Gas Mark 6/Top of the Aga Roasting Oven.
Cut the peppers, courgettes, onions and aubergines into large pieces.
Cut the tomatoes in half and together with the other vegetables add them
to a roasting tray.
Drizzle the olive oil over the vegetables and toss them in it.
Tear the herbs roughly and add these to the vegetables together with the
salt and pepper.
Roast for 40 minutes until the vegetables are charred.

**Try this accompanied with toasted ciabatta bread, hummus and grilled
hallumi cheese.**

Growing Summer Vegetables

Summer Vegetable Recipes

French Beans

French Beans (legume vegetable), usually come in the form of flat or round pods, variations in colour range from yellow, green, purple, black or mottled pods, and growth habit can range between dwarf- climbing varieties.

Sowing

Choose a sunny spot as they can be a little tender, a sheltered position, as they can be a little delicate. The climbing varieties may need protection if exposed to an open windy site. French beans can be sown from April-July.

You will have more success by sowing your seed in 6in pots filled with seed compost, two seeds per pot 5cm (2in) deep, they can be planted out when seedlings are big enough when they reach 8cm (3 in) tall, space plants 15-20cm (6-8in) apart.

Growing

French Beans need a moist fertile soil, but not too wet, you may need to protect from slugs.

Dwarf Beans are best grown in double rows or small blocks so that neighbouring plants can provide some support and protection. Climbing varieties need structural support, the simplest most traditional frame can be made from 6ft bamboo canes. A good tip is to tie in the young plants at first untill they are established, as windy weather can damage them when they are young. Once the plants have reached the top of their support, pinch out the growing tip to prevent them becoming top heavy. Any new shoots will need to be tied in to prevent a tangled mess as they develop.

Harvesting

Harvest pods as soon as they are big enough, frequent picking will encourage new growth and a prolonged cropping period.

Broad Beans

Broad beans (legume vegetable), have three main groups, long-pod (longer pods and heavy cropping), dwarf (small bushy early cropping) and Windsor (best flavour but not hardy).

Sowing

Choose a sunny spot with a sheltered position, and you may need protection from wind. Sowing seed in autumn will give you an earlier crop from Oct-Dec, alternatively, sow seed from Jan-April.

Hardy varieties can be planted straight into the ground, you can grow in one or two successional sowings to prolong the harvest. Plant Beans 5cm (2in) deep, (roughly a thumbs length), and 20cm (8in) apart. Sow in double rows with a walking space between, or blocks to aid plant support and protection. You may need to cover with mesh to protect from mice.

Growing

Keep the ground weed free and moist, you may find that you need to earth up the plants as they grow to assist with supporting them. A good tip is to support individually with canes or enclose blocks with stakes and string.

Once the first pods have set and they are flowering well, pinch off the first 8cms (3in) to discourage the black fly aphid and encourage bean formation.

Harvesting

Harvest Beans when they are small from the base of the plant and work upwards as they mature. To prevent damage to the plant use secateurs to snip the pods off from the stems.

Courgettes

A wonderful decorative ornamental addition to your allotment, a summer vegetable culinary delight that is a versatile staple, even the flowers are edible. A great plant to grow for a beginner, they are usually green or yellow in colour.

Sowing

Choose a sunny spot, and keep the ground moist, they are greedy and like to be fed well. Sow April-June.

The seeds are more successful if grown in 6in pots filled with seed compost and put on a warm windowsill or in a green house if you have one. Sow the seed on its edge 1cm (1/2in) deep. Keep moist but not too wet.

Growing

Courgettes like to be kept moist, a good tip is to water around the plant and try avoiding the crown to prevent rotting and mildew formation. They prefer a rich soil. At the end of may the seedlings are ready to be hardened off for two weeks by simply placing them outside in a warm sheltered spot during the day and bringing them in overnight. Plant out at the beginning of June.

The plants need quite a bit of room to grow, leave at least 3ft between plants. Two or three plants is all you will need as they are very productive. You may find that they need support to protect from the wind and from the weight of the crop itself which can snap the plant clean off from the base root.

Harvesting

Pick regularly when they are small and young. The more you harvest the more courgettes are produced, if you delay picking, the more likely you are to end up with marrows.

Potatoes

Potatoes are another versatile great vegetable staple. They are available in various shapes, sizes and colours, and classified as being either earlies or maincrops.

Sowing

Choose a sunny fertile spot, with good soil depth and drainage, low lying areas may be more prone to frost damage which Potatoes are susceptible to.

Purchase seed potatoes which are free from viruses, to chit from the end of Jan-March and plant them from march-May. Chit or sprout your seed Potatoes six-eight weeks prior to planting, this gives them a head start. Choose a light, cool, frost free room. Lay the seed Potato in an egg box, on its end with the eyes facing upwards.

A good tip is to plant early and maincrop potatoes at the same time. First, mark out your row with a taut garden line. Then dig a hole 15cm (6in) deep, space 30cm (12in) apart leaving 60cm (24in) between rows. Place the seed potato carefully in the hole so that you do not damage any shoots, if you have not pre fed the soil already, add an application of fertiliser and backfill and level off the soil. Identify your row with a marker.

Growing

You will need to protect your newly sprouting foliage by either covering over with a sheet or raking over soil for protection if frost is forecast. Once the plants have grown, they will need to be covered with a layer of soil, known as "earthing up," the Mattock is an ideal tool for this job. This prevents potatoes near the surface being exposed to light and turning green and poisonous, and offers some protection from the Potato Blight virus.

Harvesting

Potatoes can be ready after the flower has opened, you can delve down below the soil and feel around the roots, to find out without digging the plant up. Earlies are usually ready to harvest 10-12 weeks after planting. If they are ready, dig up carefully with a fork, moving round a few times to find any hiding tubers and then leave them to dry, before bagging in paper or hessian bags. Maincrops are usually ready when the foliage starts to yellow and droop. Maincrops usually store well in cool, dry conditions.

Onions

Onions are another great versatile vegetable staple. They are available in various shapes, sizes and colours.

Sowing

Choose a well drained sunny, open spot. Thoroughly dig over the site with a fork, removing any weeds and add a general purpose fertiliser.

They can be grown from seed, but to save time you can grow them from onion sets in spring, (Onion sets are miniature bulbs that have several weeks maturity behind them)

Mark out a row with a taut garden line, using a dibber to make a hole, plant the sets 3cm (1in) deep with the tops just showing above ground level and 13cm (5in) apart. Mark your row with a cane.

Growing

A good tip is to place a scarecrow in the onion bed, this is useful to deter the birds from pulling them out. Check every few days until growth starts and any that have been disturbed can be replanted back in their original place in the row.

Keep the soil moist during the growing period. It is important to keep them weed free as the slim tall leaves cannot shade out weeds which will compete for food and water.

Harvesting

The tops will die down in late summer which means they are ready to harvest, bend over the leaves and a few days later lift the bulbs carefully with a fork to avoid causing any damage. Dry on the surface of the ground for a few days untill the skins are dry, then rub off any loose skins and roots. You can store them in trays, nets or plait them and hang them up in a frost free place. They should store well provided you have given them the right conditions.

Tomatoes

Tomatoes are wonderful to eat straight from the vine in summer, the smell and taste are wonderful. They come in different colours, shapes and sizes, and if you choose a hardy variety, you can grow them outdoors.

Sowing

Sew seeds into a seed tray filled with seed compost in early spring and place on a warm, light, windowsill or in a greenhouse if you have one. Keep them moist but not too wet.

Growing

Once the seedlings have established and are strong enough, prick out and pot them on into individual 6in pots with more seed compost. Keep them moist, but not over wet during this early growing period. If you are growing them outside, your seedlings need a period of hardening off for two weeks at the end of May. Hardening off your plants, by simply placing them outside in a warm sheltered spot during the day and bringing them in overnight, ensures that your plants are acclimatised to the cooler temperatures outside. If you have a cold frame you can leave them in this overnight.

Your tomato plants can be planted outside in June in a sunny, sheltered spot. Dig plenty of compost into the soil prior to planting out, then create a slight well around the plant to assist in retaining moisture when watering them during the long summer months. Stake the plants and tie the stem to the support throughout the growing season. A good tip is to remove the top leaf growth when the plant has set five trusses, so that it does not become top heavy. Pinch out sucker side shoots as they form between primary and secondary stems, this will promote a good crop. Keep well watered throughout the summer and feed as per tomato feed instructions, usually from when the first truss has set (a cluster of smaller stems where flowers, then tomatoes form from, usually emerging from where a primary stem meets a secondary leaf stem)

Harvesting

Tomatoes grown outside take a little longer to ripen than greenhouse grown ones, pick them when ripe, but do not forget to smell them first!

Peas

Peas are wonderful and sweet when eaten freshly picked and cooked straight away. Pea pod shapes, sizes and colour vary with different plant varieties, and they are available in standard or dwarf forms.

Sowing

Choose a sunny, well drained spot, and provide a rich, moisture retentive soil, sowing between spring and summer, depending on the variety.

Sow peas into rows or flat trenches, 5cm (2in) deep, 5-10cm (2-4in) apart if growing in rows. A good tip if sowing in rows, is to sow double rows, this makes it easier to support them.

Growing

Provide a support system with stakes and string before the plants become top heavy and flop. Netting the plants should give some protection from pests. Water the plants if dry to keep the soil moist, especially once flowering has begun, this ensures that the pods have enough water to be able to develop properly. Mulching around the plants can be beneficial in dry spells to assist in retaining moisture.

Harvesting

Harvest from the bottom of the plant and work up. Peas can be harvested once the pods have reached a decent size, you can feel the maturity by gently sqeezing the pod to feel the firmness, if in doubt pop one open to see. They are best picked when young and sweet as they lose their flavour if left to get too big. Harvest regularly as this promotes growth and production.

After the harvest cut off the spent crops at ground level. The roots are full of nitrogen fixing material and if left to rot down in the ground they will release the nitrogen back into the soil.

French Bean and Courgette salad

Serves 4

Large handful of french beans, ends trimmed

3 Small courgettes, sliced

Large Handfull of assorted salad leaves, washed and air dried

12 Cherry tomatoes, on the vine

1 Tablespoon Olive oil

Flaky sea salt to garnish

Dressing - 2 tablespoons vegetable oil, 2 teaspoons clear honey,

2 teaspoons wholegrain mustard, 2 tablespoons lime juice

Add the olive oil to a non-stick frying pan and cook the courgettes for a few minutes until tender and browned on both sides, set aside.

Bring a pan of salted water to the boil and add the french beans, blanch for 2 minutes, drain and dunk them in to cold water to refresh, drain and pat dry.

Dry roast the tomatoes on the vine in a roasting tin for 10 minutes until browned slightly.

Add the dressing ingredients to a jam jar and shake to mix up.

Arrange the salad leaves on a plate, spread the french beans, tomatoes, and courgettes on top and drizzle the dressing on top, and finish by sprinkling flaky sea salt on top.

Try this accompanied with grilled hallumi cheese and coleslaw

Broad Bean and Mint Dip

Serves 4

300g Broad beans, shelled

3 Tablespoons Creme fraiche

Handful of mint leaves

2 Tablespoons Lime juice

Sea salt and ground black pepper

6 Pitta bread

Zest of a lime to garnish

Cook the broad beans in boiling water for 5 minutes, and leave to cool.

Chop the mint leaves finely and set aside.

In a bowl mash the broad beans roughly with a fork. You may need to peel the beans outer layer first, depending on the maturity of them, as the beans get bigger the skin gets tougher.

In a blender add the beans together with the creme fraiche, lime juice and salt and pepper and combine all the ingredients together to form a smooth consistency.

Garnish with the lime zest.

Keeps for three days in a fridge

Try this accompanied with tortilla chips, carrot and celery sticks

Roasted Courgette, Onion and Tomato Cous Cous with Chickpeas & Feta

Serves 4

3 Courgettes, 1 red onion, chopped coursley

10 Cherry tomatoes, halved

1 Large tin chickpeas, drained

Handful of mint leaves, chopped coursely

150g Feta cheese

2 Packets of lemon and coriander cous cous

Sea salt and ground black pepper

Handful of pine nut kernals

2 Tablespoons Rapeseed oil

Preheat the oven to 190 C/Gas Mark 5/Top of the Aga Roasting Oven.

Add the oil to a large roasting tin, add the courgettes, onion and tomatoes and mix together, coating them with the oil and roast for 25-30 minutes until charred and leave to cool.

Prepare the cous cous as per packet instructions and set aside.

Dry roast the pine kernals in a frying pan until slightly browned.

In a large bowl mix the cous cous, courgettes, onion, tomatoes and feta and chick peas together.

Add the mint leaves, and pine kernals, salt and pepper and mix all the ingredients together. Serve warm or cold.

Try this accompanied with hummus and toasted pitta bread

Potato and Leek Bake with Rosemary and Garlic

Serves 4

8 large new potatoes, peeled and sliced thinly

3 Leeks, outer peeled and sliced finely

250mls Boiled water

1 Vegetable stock cube

150mls Milk

1Tablespoon Rosemary leaves, chopped, 2 garlic cloves, peeled and sliced

Sea salt and ground black pepper

Preheat the oven to 180 C/Gas Mark 4/Middle of the Aga roasting Oven.

Arrange a third of the sliced potatoes to cover the bottom of a large oven proof dish, overlapping them slightly.

Scatter half of the leeks over the potatoes, reserving some for another layer.

Add another layer of potatoes overlapping them slightly.

Scatter the final layer of the leeks over the top.

Finish off with the last layer of potatoes, overlapping them slightly. Add the salt and pepper to the stock and milk, stir and pour this over the top.

Scatter the rosemary and garlic on top and finish by adding dabs of butter to the potatoes.

Cover the dish with a foil lid and cook for 1 hour, remove the lid and turn the heat up to 190C/Gas mark 5/Top of the Aga roasting oven, cook for another 20-30 minutes until tender and golden.

Try this on its own or to accompany your Sunday roast.

Roasted Onion, Pepper and Goats Cheese Tarts

Serves 6

3 Medium sized red onions, peeled and sliced lenghthways

3 Red peppers, sliced lengthways

100g Goats cheese with rind, cut into chunks

2 Tablespoons Tomato puree

Handful of basil leaves

Handful of pine kernals

1 Tablespoon Olive oil

1 Pack of puff pastry

Sea salt and ground black pepper

Preheat the oven to 190C/Gas Mark 5/Top of the Aga Roasting oven

Add the oil to a roasting tin and add the onions, peppers, salt and pepper, coat in the oil and roast for 30 minutes, and then cool.

Roll out the puff pastry and cut out tart sized circles using a saucer.

Place the pastry circles on a greased baking sheet, leave a ½ inch rim at the edge of the pastry free and prick the rest with a fork.

Mix the tomato puree and oil together and spread this on the pastry circles, arrange the onions and peppers on top, leaving ½ inch rim at the edge free, this allows the edge to puff up.

Place the goats cheese, basil leaves and pine kernals on top, add salt and pepper.

Cook for 15 minutes, until risen and golden, makes 6 tarts.

Try this accompanied wth new potatoes and french beans

Roasted Mediteranean Style Tomato Sauce

Serves 4

30 Tomatoes, halved

1 Red onion, peeled and chopped

2 Garlic cloves, peeled and sliced

A few sprigs of thyme

Handful of basil leaves

Handful of green olives

Handful of pine kernals

2 Tablespoons rapeseed oil

Sea salt and ground black pepper

Preheat the oven to 190 C/Gas mark 5/ Top of the Aga Roasting oven.

Add the oil to a roasting tin and coat the tomatoes and onion with this.

Add the thyme, basil leaves, garlic and salt and pepper and roast for 30 minutes, cool.

Liquidise the tomatoes, onion and herbs in a blender until reduced to a thick sauce consistency.

Reheat and add the olives, pine kernals and basil leaves to garnish.

Try this accompanied with roasted mediteranean vegetables and pasta

Pea, Mint, and Feta Cheese Frittatas

Serves 4

150g Shelled peas
5 Large eggs
125g Feta cheese, crumbled
4-5 Spring onion bulbs, chopped finely
4 Tablespoons Milk
6 Sprigs of fresh mint, chopped roughly
Sea salt and ground black pepper
A few sprigs of flat leaf parsley, chopped
Butter to grease muffin tin

Preheat the oven to 200 C/Gas mark 6/Top of the Aga roasting oven.
Place the peas in a pan of boiling water and cook for 5 minutes, then drain.
Beat the eggs together with the cream in a bowl and then combine with the
peas, spring onions, crumbled feta, salt and pepper and chopped mint.
Grease a muffin tin with butter.
Add the mixture to each muffin hole, leaving a gap at the top edge for
room for expansion and once the holes are filled transfer to the oven.
Bake for 10-15 minutes, until puffed and golden, makes 8 muffins.
Garnish with the chopped parsley to finish, serve hot or cold.

Try this accompanied with a mixed leaf salad and potato salad

Growing Autumn Vegetables

Autumn Vegetable Recipes

Beetroot

Beetroot is available in a variety of colours, red, yellow, white or bicoloured and varies in root shapes which can be flat, round or tapering, and is especially delicious roasted, steamed or pickled.

Sowing

Choose a sunny or partial shady spot that is well drained, apply a general fertiliser to the site you are planning to sow into a few weeks prior to sowing. A good tip is to sow when it is warm as the seeds will germinate readily, if it is cool outside you can always start them off in a seed tray and plant out when large enough to handle.

Sow late spring/late summer. Using the back of your hoe make a drill and sow seeds 2.5cm (1in) deep, 30cm (12in) apart and water well. Mark the row with a line marker.

Growing

Once the seedlings have grown and become established, you can thin them out if you wish, this will allow the beetroot room so that they can grow bigger. Alternatively if you leave them they will be overall smaller in size and you will end up with more of a variety of sizes.

Keep them moist and weed free during the growing period.

Harvesting

Beetroot are especially delicious small, I prefer picking mine when they are small as the flavour is sweeter. Start harvesting when they are small for steaming and roasting. The larger ones are perfect for steaming and pickling.

They will store dry after twisting the leaves off and keep for a few weeks until ready for use.

Butternut Squash

Butternut squash are a very decorative groundcover crop. They look so majestic when they are rambling through other crops and their uses are so versatile in cooking. They are wonderful roasted, steamed or blended into dips or soups.

Sowing

Sow mid spring/early summer into individual three inch pots of seed compost. Sow seeds on their edge, ½ inch deep, and water in. Keep them moist but not over wet in a greenhouse. At the end of May the seedlings are ready to be hardened off for two weeks by simply placing in a sheltered spot during the day and bringing them in overnight. Plant out at the beginning of June.

Growing

Choose an open, sunny, well drained, sheltered spot with enough room for them to grow. Squashes can be grown in between crops. As they provide ground cover as they ramble, a good tip is to grow them in between tall plants such as sweetcorn and tomatoes.

Prepare the area which you are planning to use to plant out your squash seedlings, by adding a general fertiliser a few weeks beforehand. Dig out a large hole and fill with compost and mix with the excavated soil to plant your seedlings into, leave a slight mound to assist with watering them. Keep well watered in dry weather.

Harvesting

When the squashes are large enough and starting to change colour, a good tip to assist the ripening process is to place the squash on top of one of the attatched leaves on the ground and create an opening in the leaves around the squash to expose them to the sunlight.

Harvest before the autumn frosts, cutting the stem two inches from the base of the squash to aid storage. Complete ripening their skins by placing them in full sun on a table for a week or two, store in a dry, frost free shed.

Broccoli

Broccoli is a handsome delicious vegetable that is available in a couple of forms, sprouting or large head varieties and has green, white or purple coloured spears. It is good roasted, steamed or made into soups or dips.

Sowing

Choose a sunny, well drained, sheltered spot.

Sow mid spring/early summer into a nursery bed or tray filled with seed compost. When seedlings are large enough to handle you can transplant them into their final position.

Growing

Prepare a bed prior to planting out the seedlings beforehand by adding a general fertiliser and rake over the area to produce a fine crumbly texture. Firm the bed by walking up and down the bed several times.

Leave 30cm (12in) between large head varieties and 45cm (18in) between sprouting varieties.

When transplanting the seedlings ensure that the plant is planted up to the first leaf formation and firm well into the ground. A good tip is to firm the plants in at each weeding session and earth up if necessary for anchorage. These plants can become top heavy and develop wind rock which can affect the root formation.

Provide protection from pests by staking and netting the bed during the growing season. Keep well watered as this does assist in preventing bolting of the crop.

Harvesting

Harvest broccoli when the heads are well formed and tight before the flowers open. Pick them regularly and this will encourage side shoot growth and further harvests and extend the cropping time.

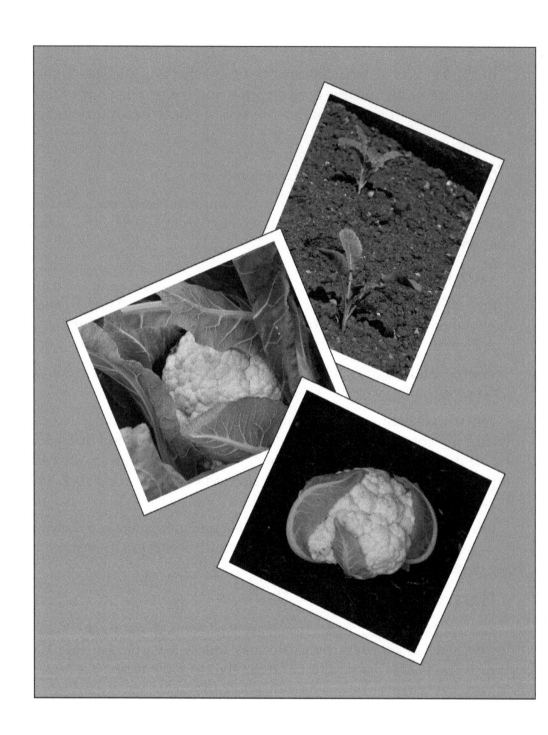

Cauliflower

Cauliflower is a versatile and ornamental vegetable which has different shaped heads and colours which vary from white and purple to lime green. There are miniature and standard varieties available. It is especially delicious roasted, steamed or pickled.

Sowing

Choose a sunny, open spot with moisture retentive soil. To aid the soils moisture-holding capacity you can dig in plenty of manure in autumn which will break down over winter.

Sow mid-late spring in a prepared nursery bed or a tray filled with seed compost. When seedlings are large enough to handle you can transplant them into their final position.

Growing

Prepare a bed prior to planting out the seedlings beforehand by adding a general fertiliser and rake over the area to produce a fine crumbly texture. Firm the soil by walking up and down the bed several times.

Leave 60cm (24in) between seedlings.

When transplanting the seedlings ensure that the plant is planted up to the first leaf formation and firm well into the ground. A good tip is to firm the plants in at each weeding session and earth up if necessary for anchorage.

Provide protection from pests by staking and netting the bed during the growing season. Keep them well watered as this does assist in preventing bolting of the crop.

During the growing season to prevent the head from being discoloured from the sunlight, bend a couple of the uppermost leaves over the head to protect it.

Harvesting

Harvest cauliflower when the heads are well formed, tight and small, before the heads seperate.

Sweetcorn

Sweetcorn is delicious freshly picked and barbecued with lots of butter melted on top, a treat for sure.

Sowing

Choose a sheltered, well drained, sunny spot, dress the site you are planning to prepare with a general fertiliser. Sow in late spring. Sweetcorn does not like cold and frosts and does better sown indoors and planted out when all danger of frost has gone.

Sow each seed kernel into a small pot or root module to avoid root disturbance when planting out the seedlings.

Growing

Once the seedlings are big enough and all threat of frosts have gone, harden the seedlings off a few weeks prior to transplanting out. Hardening off your plants, by simply placing them outside in a warm sheltered spot during the day and bringing them in overnight, ensures that your plants are acclimatised to the cooler temperatures outside.

Plant the seedlings in the ground 45cm (18in) apart in a block formation, which will provide the best possible conditions for successful wind pollination. A good tip is to earth up as they can get top heavy and provide support in windy conditions.

The male flowers shower pollen down from the top of the plant to the females below, the pollen is less likely to be blown away when grown in this way. Water well when the kernels are swelling.

Harvesting

Sweetcorn matures from midsummer onwards, you can start to test for maturity once the tassels on the end of the cobs start to turn brown. Simply peel back the husk that covers the cob, just a little bit, to reveal the corn, it will be pale yellow when ready to be picked. To test for maturity dig your nail into one of the kernels, if it is ripe a milky liquid will appear. Pick by twisting the cob from the main stem, cook as soon after picking for a delicious sweet taste.

Roasted Beetroot with Baked Goats Cheese, Walnuts and Honey

Serves 4

4 Small beetroots, washed with skins on, cut into chunks
4 Individual portion goats cheese with skins on
2 Tablespoons Runny honey
A large handful of walnuts
Zest of an orange
2 Tablespoons Rapeseed oil

Preheat the oven to 200C/ Gas Mark 6/ Top of the Aga Oven.
Put the oil in a roasting tin and place the beetroot in it and coat evenly, roast for 15- 20 minutes until slightly charred.
Place the goats cheese rounds on a baking tray lined with grease proof paper, drizzle the honey over the top and roast for 10-12 minutes until soft and browned, set aside.
Dry toast the walnuts until slightly browned in a frying pan, set aside.
Plate up the goats cheese and scatter the walnuts on top, with the beetroot on the side and the orange zest scattered on top of the beetroot pieces.

Try this accompanied with a mixed leaf salad and new potatoes

Spiced Butternut Squash and Chickpea Filo Tarts

Serves 4-6

2 Large butternut squash, skin on, washed and chopped roughly

1 Tin of coconut milk, 1 tin chickpeas drained

1 Tablespoon Rapeseed oil

1 Tablespoon Madras paste

100mls water

1 Packet filo pastry sheets

100g Butter, melted

Sea salt and ground black pepper

Handful thyme leaves and seseme seeds

Preheat the oven 190 C/Gas Mark 5/Top of the Aga Roasting Oven.

Place half the butternut squash, water, coconut milk, madras paste, salt and pepper in a pan and bring to a slow simmer, cook for 15 minutes until soft, cool then liquidise with a stick blender until a thick sauce consistency, this forms the filling, mix in the chickpeas.

Place the other half of the butternut squash in a roasting tin and coat with the oil and roast for 30-40 minutes until soft and charred, set aside.

Melt the butter in a pan until it becomes liquid. Brush each sheet of filo pastry with the butter and arrange overlapping each sheet into individual greased tart tins, scrunching the edges.

Fill the tart tins with the butternut squash filling, topped with the roast butternut squash and goats cheese, cook for 10-15 minutes until the pastry is lightly browned. Garnish with thyme and seseme seeds.

Try this accompanied with a cous cous salad

Broccoli and Blue Cheese Soup

Serves 4

300g Broccoli together with leaves, chopped

150g Blue cheese, crumbled

2 Onions, peeled and chopped

2 Potatoes, peeled and chopped

2 Tablespoons Rapeseed oil

2 Litres water

1 Vegetable stock cube

4 Tablespoons double cream

Sea salt and ground black pepper to taste

Heat the oil in a pan and cook the potatoes and onions for 2 minutes.

Add the broccoli and cover the pan and sweat for 10 minutes.

Add the vegetable stock, and salt and pepper and stir.

Bring all the ingredients to the boil and simmer for 15-20 minutes, until soft.

Cool slightly then add the cream and cheese before liquidising with a stick blender to a smooth consistency.

Reheat and serve with blue cheese crumbled on top.

Try this accompanied with chunky ciabatta bread wedges

Roasted Spicy Cauliflower

Serves 4

Cauliflower head, seperate the florets

3 Teaspoons Coriander seeds

3 Teaspoons fennel seeds

1 Teaspoon Dried red chillies

3 Teaspoons Dried thyme

1 Teaspoon Salt

1 Teaspoon Ground black pepper

2 Cloves of garlic, peeled and crushed

2 Tablespoons Rapeseed oil

Preheat the oven 200 C/ Gas mark 6/ Top of the Aga roasting oven

Wash the cauliflower and pat dry with kitchen paper.

Put all the spices, herbs and salt and pepper into a pestle and mortar and pound them up to make a powder consistency.

Add the garlic and pound it into the spices.

Scoop the spices into a bowl and add the oil and combine this together to form a paste.

Coat the cauliflower in the spice paste on both sides.

Roast in a roasting tin for 30-40 minutes until brown and crispy.

Try this accompanied with cous cous salad or as a vegetable for your Sunday roast

Sweetcorn Fritters

Serves 4

3 Large sweetcorn cobs, kernals cut from the cobs

4 Heaped tablespoons cornflour

3 Spring onions, chopped finely

1 Red chilli, deseeded and chopped finely

2 Tablespoons Rapeseed oil

A large handful of flat leaf parsley, chopped finely

Sea salt and ground black pepper

4-5 Tablespoons Double cream

Mix together in a bowl the sweetcorn, spring onions, parsley, chilli and salt and pepper.

Mix together in a small bowl the cream and cornflour until smooth, it should be a batter consistency, add this to the sweetcorn mixture and mix well.

Heat the oil in a frying pan and add a spoonful at a time of the sweetcorn mixture, add no more than 4 to the pan at one time, so that they cook through.

Cook for 4-5 minutes on each side until lightly golden and crisp.

Drain on kitchen towel and serve garnished with parsley.

Makes 8 fritters.

Try this accompanied with sour cream and a mixed leaf salad

Growing Winter Vegetables

Winter Vegetable Recipes

Kale

Kale will add an ornamental and decorative quality to your plot. There are several groups with curly, plain, rape, leaf and spear varieties. It is very versatile and is one of the most attractive and tastiest of the brassica family. It is especially delicious steamed or stir-fryed which retains more of the natural flavour.

Sowing

Choose a sheltered, sunny or partial shady spot.

Sow spring to early summer into modules filled with seed compost or into a seedbed. Prepare the bed a couple of weeks beforehand by digging in a general fertiliser and raking the soil to a fine crumbly texture.

Growing

Transplant the seedlings when they are big enough to handle, approximately 6-8 weeks after sowing into their final position. Plant 45cm (18in) apart. Plant the seedlings into the ground to a depth up to the first set of leaves and firm well in.

Water well and keep well watered throughout the growing period, especially during dry spells. A good tip is to stake the plants to support them during the growing period.

You do not need to worry during cold spells as kale is completely frost hardy.

Harvesting

Remove any yellowing leaves during the growing period, to deter any diseases. Young leaves can be picked right through from autumn to spring.

Harvest leaves while the leaves are still young and tender, as the plant ages, the leaves become tougher and bitter. Start by cutting the leaves with a knife from the crown of the plant and work outwards. This will encourage the plant to produce side shoots and bush out.

Carrots

Carrots are one of the most tasty, versatile and delicious winter root crops to grow, they are wonderful in soups, dips, roasted, or eaten raw. They are available in various colours and root shapes and sizes, and they are classified as early or maincrop varieties.

Sowing

Choose a well drained, fertile spot, add compost and sand into the soil to lighten it if you have a clay based soil which will aid the root growth.

Dig the area over a couple of weeks prior to sowing to get a good depth, adding in a general fertiliser at the same time.

Sow spring through to summer outdoors or in seed trays to start off if the weather is cool, seeds germinate quicker if the soil is warm.

Rake the soil to a fine crumbly texture and then mark out a row with a line marker and make a seed drill with the side of your hoe 1cm (1/2in) deep 15cm (6in) between rows, sow thinly, cover with soil and firm down. Water the seeds in and mark the end of the row with a stick.

Growing

You may need to thin out the seedlings if the seeds were not sown thinly, try to avoid this as it will attract the carrot root fly. A good tip is to provide a barrier with fine mesh around your carrots from late spring to summer, attached to stakes or a tunnel system to stop the carrot root fly from laying its eggs next to your plants, the larvae then tunnel into and eat the carrots.

Water during dry spells and when the foliage begins to wilt and keep them weed free.

Harvesting

Harvest them when big enough by lifting with a small fork to prevent damage to the root.

If you like small carrots, pick them when they are young, these can be lifted by hand if the soil is soft enough.

Carrots can be lifted and stored in boxes of sand and stored in a shed, it is worth noting that this does affect the quality of flavour though.

Parsnips

Parsnips are a wonderful winter rootcrop to grow, they are especially good in soups, stews, roasted, chipped or pureed. They are available in different root shapes and sizes.

Sowing

Choose a sunny, well drained spot. Add compost and sand into the soil to lighten it if you have a clay based soil which will aid the root growth.

Dig the area over a couple of weeks prior to sowing to get a good depth, adding in a general fertiliser at the same time.

Sow early to late spring outdoors, rake the soil to a fine crumbly texture then mark out a row with a line marker and using the side of your hoe make a drill 1cm (1/2in) deep 30cm (12in) between rows. A good tip is to water the drill initially, the seeds are light and flyaway and this will enable them to stick to the soil making it easier to sow them. Cover with soil and firm down. Water the seeds in and mark the end of the row with a stick.

Growing

You may need to thin the seedlings out if the seeds were not sown thinly this aids the maturity and development of the root growth.

Parsnips do not need a lot of watering and are generally drought tolerant, only water them if the foliage wilts and keep them weed free.

Harvesting

You can start harvesting young parsnips in late summer by lifting them with a fork to reduce damage to the root.

It is the cold weather and frosts in particular that give the parsnips their characteristic sweet flavour turning the starch into sugars. They are at their best after the frosts have arrived. They can be left in the ground until needed, let the foliage die back with the frosts and you can be sure that the parsnips will be tasty and sweet.

Parsnips can be lifted and stored in boxes of sand and stored in a shed.

Leeks

Leeks are a useful winter vegetable staple especially for hearty stews and casseroles, also delicious roasted with other root vegetables. They are available with different root sizes and disease resistant varieties to rust and canker.

Sowing

Choose a sunny, well drained spot that does not become water logged in winter.

Sow the seeds into a prepared seed bed or into seed trays containing seed compost before pricking out and planting out when they are big enough into their final growing position.

Rake the soil over and add in a general fertiliser at the same time a week before transplanting the leeks. The leeks are ready to transplant when they are the thickness of a pencil. Mark out a row with a line marker and make holes with a dibber 15cm (6in) deep and 5cm (2in) across along the row. Drop a single seedling into each hole and backfill with water only to settle the soil around the roots. This will produce white shafts of good length.

Growing

Ensure that you keep the leeks weed free using a hoe gently in between rows, being careful not to damage the leaves or roots as they are growing.

A good tip is to earth up the leeks gradually, piling soil around the shafts during the growing season, this will encourage the shafts to grow longer. Water during dry spells.

Harvesting

Leeks are ready to harvest when the stems have thickened up, lift earlier if you prefer young baby ones. Lift with a fork and trim the roots and leaves with a knife.

Wash them thoroughly before use as the soil can become trapped between and inside the leaf layers. Leeks are best eaten fresh as they do not store well.

Kale Macaroni Cheese Bake

Serves 4

A Large handful of kale leaves, stalks removed and chopped coursley

350g Macaroni

75g Guryere cheese, grated

50g Parmesan cheese, grated

Sauce ingredients- 75g Butter, 4 tablespoons Plain flour, 750mls Milk, sea salt and ground black pepper

Preheat the oven to 200 C/Gas Mark 6/Top of the Aga Roasting oven.

In a pan melt the butter, add the flour and stir to make a smooth paste, remove from the heat then gradually add the milk a little at a time stirring continuously with a wooden spoon, return to the heat and cook for a few minutes until it thickens and becomes smooth and shiny.

Add the guryere cheese and stir in.

Fill a large pan with water, season with salt and bring to the boil, add the macaroni and simmer for 6 minutes and then drain.

 Add the sauce and kale to the pan of macaroni and combine together. Place the combined ingredients in an ovenproof dish and cook for 20 minutes until golden brown. Sprinkle with grated parmesan and serve.

Try this accompanied with a mixed leaf salad

Carrot and Lentil Soup

Serves 4

8 Large carrots, washed and chopped

1 Large onion, finely chopped

2 Garlic cloves, peeled and finely chopped

1 Red chilli, deseeded and finely chopped

4 Tomatoes, roughly chopped

150g Red lentils

2 litres water, 2 vegetable stock cubes

Sea salt and ground black pepper

1 Tablespoon Rapeseed oil

Juice of a lemon

Handful of flat leaf parsley

Heat the oil in a large pan, add the onion and carrots and cook for 3-4 minutes without browning until soft.

Add the garlic and chilli and cook for 2 minutes.

Add the tomatoes, lentils, stock cube and water and bring to the boil.

Reduce the heat and simmer for 20-25 minutes until the lentils are soft.

Cool slightly and then liquidise with a stick blender to a smooth consistency, add salt and pepper and lemon juice.

Serve warmed, garnished with parsley.

Try this accompanied with a crusty french stick

Parsnip, Pear, and Goats Cheese Quiche

Serves 6

4 Parsnips, peeled and chopped

1 Onion, peeled and chopped finely

2 Pears, peeled, cored and sliced

100g Goats cheese log, sliced into circles

75g Parmesan cheese, grated

1 Pack of pre-rolled shortcrust pastry

1 Tablespoon Runny honey

100mls Single cream

4 Eggs, beaten

2 Tablespoons Rapeseed oil

Handful of thyme leaves

Sea salt and ground black pepper

Preheat the oven to 190 C /Gas Mark 5/ Top of Aga Roasting oven.

Place the parsnips in a pan of boiling water and simmer for 5 minutes, drain and place in a roasting tin with the pears, onion salt and pepper, coat with the oil and honey and roast for 20 minutes, set aside.

Place the pastry in a greased 8 in quiche tin, prick the bottom with a fork and bake blind for 12 minutes by adding greaseproof paper inside with baking beans in the centre to weigh the paper down.

Place the roasted parsnip mixture in the pastry case and scatter the goats cheese and thyme over the top, add the cream, and parmesan to the eggs and mix well and pour this over the top, cook for 30 minutes until set and golden brown.

Try this accompanied with potato salad and cous cous

Leek and Potato Soup

Serves 4

4 large leeks, washed and chopped, reserve a handful for garnishing

1 Large onion, peeled and chopped

2 Medium potatoes, peeled and chopped

50g Butter

1 Tablespoon Rapeseed oil

1 litre water,

1 Vegetable stock cube

250mls Milk

Sea salt and ground black pepper

Melt the butter in a large pan and add the leeks, potatoes, onions and salt and pepper.

Coat all the vegetables with the butter, cover the pan with a lid, and sweat over a low heat for 15 minutes.

Add the water, stock cube and milk, bring to a gentle simmer.

Simmer for 15-20 minutes until soft, remove from the heat and cool slightly.

Meanwhile put the reserved leeks in a frying pan and coat with the oil and fry for 5 minutes until brown and crispy.

Liquidise the leek mix with a stick blender to a smooth consistency, reheat and serve warmed, garnished with the crispy leeks

Try this accompanied with a buttered cheese scone

Acknowledgements

Firstly a big thankyou to Brian my husband, for his brilliant technical skills and support, and for running me a bath when I have needed one, I love you, you are my rock and soulmate.

Also a big thankyou to Ben, a friend and neighbour, who loaned me part of his allotment, which fuelled my interest and enabled my allotment bug to grow.

Thankyou to Andrew at Norwell Nurseries for inspiring me to grow asparagus and for always being friendly and free with his advice.

Thankyou to all my allotment neighbours and friends who are a lovely bunch of allotment addicts with whom I can share chats and cups of tea with and for being willing to test my recipes.

Resources

Recommended seed suppliers

Thompson and Morgan https://www.thompson-morgan.com

The Organic Gardening catalogue www.organiccatalog.com

Suttons https://www.suttons.co.uk

Mr Fothergills https://www.mr-fothergills.co.uk

The sowing times, seed and planting information is for advice only, refer to the specific instructions given on the back of seed packets.

Further Reading

Clawson, Hose, and Harby Neighbourhood Plan 2017-2036 Regulation 14 Consultation.

Clevely Andi, The Allotment Book, Harper Collins, 2006

Evelegh Tessa, The Big Allotment Challenge,

Hodder & Stroughton, 2014

Klein Carol, Grow Your Own Veg, Octopus Publishing Group, 2007

Petherick Tom, Sufficient, Pavillion Books, 2007

Photographs

Brian Hiley

Lightning Source UK Ltd.
Milton Keynes UK
UKHW051221100223
416601UK00003B/164